ANIMALS AT WORK

Animals
Living in Groups

WORLD
BOOK

World Book, Inc.
180 North LaSalle Street
Suite 900
Chicago, Illinois 60601
USA

Produced for World Book, Inc. by Bailey Publishing Associates Ltd.

For information about other World Book publications, visit our website at **www.worldbook.com** or call **1-800-WORLDBK (967-5325).**

Library of Congress Cataloging-in-Publication data has been applied for.

Title: Animals Living in Groups
ISBN: 978-0-7166-2733-3

Animals at Work
ISBN: 978-0-7166-2724-1 (set, hc)

Also available as:
ISBN: 978-0-7166-2746-3 (e-book)

Printed in China by Shenzhen Wing King Tong Paper Products Co, Ltd., Shenzhen, Guangdong
1st printing August 2018

4361

Staff

Writer: Mary Auld

Executive Committee

President
Jim O'Rourke

Vice President and Editor in Chief
Paul A. Kobasa

Vice President, Finance
Donald D. Keller

Vice President, Marketing
Jean Lin

Vice President, International
Maksim Rutenberg

Vice President, Technology
Jason Dole

Director, Human Resources
Bev Ecker

Editorial

Director, Print Publishing
Tom Evans

Managing Editor
Jeff De La Rosa

Editor
William D. Adams

Manager, Contracts & Compliance
(Rights & Permissions)
Loranne K. Shields

Manager, Indexing Services
David Pofelski

Librarian
S. Thomas Richardson

Digital

Director, Digital Product Development
Erika Meller

Digital Product Manager
Jonathan Wills

Manufacturing/Production

Manufacturing Manager
Anne Fritzinger

Proofreader
Nathalie Strassheim

Graphics and Design

Senior Art Director
Tom Evans

Senior Designer
Don Di Sante

Media Editor
Rosalia Bledsoe

Special thanks to:

Roberta Bailey
Nicola Barber
Francis Paola Lea
Claire Munday
Alex Woolf

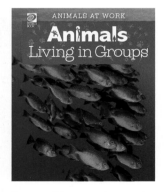

Common bigeyes swim together in a shoal. Many animals gather in groups for protection from predators.

Acknowledgments

Cover photo: © Rich Carey, Shutterstock

Alamy: 5 (Rolf Hicker/All Canada Photos), 10 (Bill Gozansky), 12-13 (AfriPics.com), 14-15 (Chris Gomersall), 16-17 (blickwinkel), 21 (WILDLIFE GmbH), 22 (Gillian Pullinger), 22-23 (Rob Sheppard/DanitaDelimont.com), 23 (Michael Durham/Minden Pictures), 25 (Michio Hoshino), 26-27 (Natural Selection Bill Byrne/Design Pics Inc), 29 (Jack Jeffrey/Photo Resource Hawaii), 30-31 (Robert McGouey/Wildlife), 34-35 (Laura Romin & Larry Dalton), 35 (Matthias Graben/imageBROKER), 36-37 (Anup Shah/Nature Picture Library), 37 (Nigel Dennis/imageBROKER), 38-39 (Mark Wardle), 42-43 (Morley Read), 43 (blickwinkel/Schmidbauer). **Shutterstock:** title page & 40-41 (Victor Tyakht), 6-7 (kaschibo), 7 (Fabian Plock), 8 (JMx Images), 9 (Franke de Jong), 10-11 (lightrain), 11 (Richard Whitcombe), 12 (Martha Marks), 15 (Giedriius), 16 (Dave Pusey), 17 (noppadon sangpeam), 18-19 (Alexandr Junek Imaging), 19 (sidneydealmeida), 24-25 (Bob Hilscher), 27 (Albin Ebert), 28-29 (Brandon B), 31 (PRILL), 33 (Michael Potter11), 39 (wildestanimal), 41 (Iryna Rasko), 42 (Ivan Marjanovic), 45 (Piotr Gatlik).

Contents

Introduction

Think about the community in which you live. You may live near dozens, if not thousands or even millions, of other people. You probably see and talk to some of those people each day. Everyone depends on other people in their community. For example, farmers grow food for many people, and workers take care of the networks that provide homes with power and water. Almost everyone has friends or family that they are close with. Living in groups is part of what has made humans so successful.

Many animals also live in groups. Some groups are small: perhaps two parents and their young. Some are huge: an **insect colony** can be made up of over a million individuals. Sometimes these groups contain a mixture of animal **species,** such as some fish **shoals,** but many are made up of a single species. Some groups are temporary—they last for a short time. Others last for many generations. There are many animals that live alone most of the time. Few **mollusks** and **reptiles** live in groups, for example, even though they may live in the same area. But most animals gather together in groups for at least part of their lives.

So why do animals form groups? The simplest answer is to survive. By living in a group, animals can improve their chances of finding food, avoiding **predators, mating,** and raising their young. All of these things help a species survive.

Animals from the same species that live together—including humans—are called social animals. Social animals have different ways of living together. Some **social structures,** such as a herd of grazing animals, are looser than others, formed to find food and avoid danger. Other social structures are more organized, with a strict **dominance hierarchy,** such as groups of chimpanzees.

Social animals depend on each other for their survival. Sometimes, animals from the group take on such specific roles that only a few members **reproduce.** Animals that form such highly structured groups are called **eusocial** (*yew SOH shuhl)* animals.

In this book, you will read about how and why animals live in groups, especially social animals. You will discover the advantages and disadvantages (pluses and minuses) of group living, and how animals have developed ways of functioning a group. Finally, you will learn about the complex societies of eusocial animals.

Sea otters gather in groups called rafts for safety. They hold front paws in the water to keep from drifting apart as they sleep.

Group Benefits

There are many collective names for groups of animals: a flock of birds, a herd of antelope, a **shoal** of fish. Groups are a common part of the animal world. Group living has several benefits, the most important being protection.

LOOKING OUT FOR DANGER

One big advantage of living in a group is that there are more animals to watch for danger. With so many animals watching for **predators,** each one can spend less time looking around and more time eating. In a grazing herd, the animals on the outside of the group are most likely to spot danger first. They raise the alarm about a possible predator, and the whole group moves away from it. When a shoal of fish feeds in a coral reef, members of the group know there is danger around if one or two of them suddenly dart away.

While many herds of animals live on open grasslands, other smaller groups live in forests, finding food in the treetops or on the forest floor. The branches may hide them from predators, but they also make it harder to spot approaching danger. Where a group is feeding together, such as a flock of parrots or a family of monkeys, it only takes one member to spot a bird of prey circling above them or a panther climbing up from below. The lookout's calls quickly tell the rest of the group of the threat.

Lookout posts

Some groups of animals, such as those of meerkats, prairie dogs, and baboons, post lookouts at places around their **territory,** such as a tall hill, to watch for danger. A baboon lookout barks when it spots dangerous predators coming near the group.

A baboon sits on an exposed tree branch to watch for predators.

Shoals of feeding fish move slowly. They are alerted to danger by one of them moving quickly.

SEEKING SAFETY

When under attack, a **prey** animal's instinct—something it is born knowing how to do—is to move towards the center of the group. The center of the group is the safest place to be most of the time, so animals move toward it even when they are not being attacked. This habit helps keep a group together, whether it is a grazing herd or a **shoal** of fish.

Groups offer extra protection against **predators** for their strong, fit members. When predators attack a group, they kill the first animals they can reach. These victims are more likely to be the slow, sick, old, or young members of a group. As a result, the fast, healthy individuals are more likely to survive and **reproduce.**

CAUSING CONFUSION

Groups attract predators, which puts their members in danger. But the nature of a large group brings more protection than just the early sighting of danger. Predators can be confused when they see a large group of the same type of animal, all about the same color and size. The group creates its own **camouflage,** with each animal blending into another. A predator is confused and finds it difficult to target its prey.

This camouflage effect grows when the animals are moving. In a large group, the swirling movement of similar-looking individuals makes them even harder to tell apart. Even when a predator can identify an individual to target, the movement of other animals around the potential prey animal distracts the predator during the chase. Zebras, who range in herds of up to a hundred across the **savanna,** have black and white stripes that are especially good at camouflaging individuals in the group.

Gaming experiment

Birds called starlings gather in huge flocks called murmurations. Their amazing, shape-changing group flights are often seen over cities at dusk. Scientists have created a 3D computer game showing the movement of the birds. Human players, acting as flying predators, try to catch a single bird. The results showed that the confusion effect works in large groups. The larger the murmuration, the harder a player found it to single out and catch an individual bird.

A murmuration of starlings makes group flying movements.

It is hard to pick out one zebra from a moving herd.

MOVING IN A GROUP

Animals moving in a group can sometimes move faster than they could as individuals. For swimming or flying animals, the leader reduces **drag** for the animals following it, helping them save energy. Geese form V-shaped groups when they fly: apart from the leader, each bird flies behind another in such a way that cuts down drag. The birds take turns leading, so no one individual becomes too tired and the group keeps up its speed. Traveling in a group can even save land animals energy. When caribou migrate, they form single-file lines. The leader breaks through the deep snow, making it easier for others to follow its path.

KEEPING TOGETHER

When one animal in a group moves in a particular direction, it is natural for others to follow. Animals' fast reactions help them change direction quickly. A single animal can set off a wave of movement that travels far faster than the actual animals. In fish, this wave crosses a **school** five to ten times faster than any of its members can swim. Scientists studying animal group movement have learned that an animal responds to the actions of its nearest neighbors. When a group of starlings is flying (see page 9), each bird can see about six or seven birds around it.

Red-billed queleas (KWEE lee uhz) flying in flocks respond to the movements of their near neighbors.

A V-shaped flight of geese is called a skein (skayn).

Shoals and schools

A **shoal** of fish describes any group of fish; a school is a group of fish all moving in the same direction. The sardine run (see page 39) is an example of a school of fish. Schooling enables the fish to move through the water at great speed. Predatory fish called barracudas will sometimes form schools so they are better able to hunt sardines.

Barracudas are fast ocean predators. They move even faster in a school.

FORAGING GROUPS

Group living helps some animals find food more easily. Because of the safety of the group, grazing animals (which have to eat a lot each day) can focus on eating rather than constantly watching for danger. Even though each member of the group spends less time watching for **predators,** they are still safer than they would be if alone.

HUNTING IN A PACK

Group hunting helps meat-eating animals. Working together during a hunt allows groups to catch larger **prey** than the animals could if each hunted alone. For example, a pack of several wolves, each the size of a large dog, may hunt down an adult bison, weighing 1,600 pounds (730 kilograms) or more. The wolves work together to separate a single animal from its group. The pack then can surround and attack the prey animal. African wild dogs are strong pack hunters. They will chase such prey animals as antelope for miles or kilometers. After a while, the prey tires and the pack moves in for the kill.

Mammals are the best-known pack hunters, but many kinds of animals use this method as well. Huge **swarms** of army ants kill animals many times their size. Groups of crocodiles and alligators work to drive prey animals towards each other, so they can be caught and killed. Some **species** of fish also hunt in packs. Harris hawks, desert birds of prey, work together to hunt. Hawks on the ground work to drive a prey animal out of hiding places, while others perch on plants waiting to swoop down and catch the prey as it tries to get away.

A Harris hawk perches on a cactus, watching for its prey.

African wild dogs are small, but when they hunt as a pack they can kill large prey.

Social Structures

Different social animals have different **social structures.** All group members may be more or less equal, or a single individual may be the most important in the group.

PART OF THE CROWD

Large groups of animals will often be made up of a number of smaller groups. Bird **colonies,** for example, are made up of many families, which are in turn made up of one or two parents and their chicks. Each family has a nest in the colony and defends a small **territory** around it. Rooks, a type of crow, nest together in colonies called rookeries, with pairs usually staying together for life. Young rooks form independent **foraging** groups, but they return to the same rookery to raise their own families when they get older.

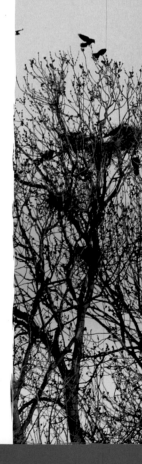

DIFFERENT PARTS TO PLAY

For some pack hunters, an animal's position in the group may help decide its part in the hunt. Males and females might have different jobs in the hunt, for instance. In wolves, the faster, lighter females run around the **prey,** driving it toward the larger males who make the kill. Female lions often hunt in packs, while males usually hunt alone. The jobs that animals have in a group often strengthen its hierarchies. When chimpanzees hunt, older, **dominant** males often set up ambushes, forcing prey back toward a chasing group. The dominant males get the largest share of the meat.

Within the herd

Some herds of grazing animals are made up of family groups. In the Arctic winter, musk oxen live in herds of several dozen for safety and warmth. But the herd splits into smaller groups in the summer. Each group contains a dominant male and several females along with their young calves. The male **mates** with all the females in his **harem** and drives away other males.

Large, adult musk oxen can protect their young from predators.

Rooks build their rookeries high in the tree branches.

FAMILY GROUPS

Smaller groups are often made up of only a single family. Adult male and female elephants live separately most of the time, although they live in the same area and will meet to **mate.** The females live in family groups of around 10 animals, including three or four adult females, newborn calves, and young elephants. The oldest female, often called a **matriarch,** leads the group and helps it find food and water.

STRONG FEMALES

Spotted hyenas form large packs called clans. A female leads the clan: she eats first at a kill and will make sure her offspring eat well, too. Her good diet keeps her healthy and helps her **reproduce** successfully. She mates with several males, choosing her partners after they perform a **submissive,** bowing display (show). One of her daughters usually takes over the clan leadership when the mother dies.

MALE DOMINANCE

Dominant males lead lion groups, which are called prides. They come into the group from the outside, but the females are usually related. Males arriving in a pride often try to kill cubs so they can mate with the lionesses. A female cannot become pregnant while she is nursing her cubs. She can only reproduce again when the cubs grow up or if they die. The lionesses of a pride will jointly defend their cubs from these attacks, but adult males still cause about a quarter of all cub deaths.

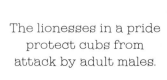

The lionesses in a pride protect cubs from attack by adult males.

Pecking orders

Social structures based on the dominance of one animal over another are called **dominance hierarchies.** In some dominance hierarchies, every animal has a place above or below another one. These are called linear (LIHN ee uhr) hierarchies. They are found in chickens: one for the males of a group and another for the females. The birds form these hierarchies by fighting with or pecking at one another, so they are sometimes called pecking orders.

Red junglefowl are wild chickens. A large rooster will head up the male pecking order.

The oldest female leads an elephant herd.

PARENTAL CONTROL

Wolf packs are mostly family groups, although sometimes outsiders are allowed to join them. A pack is usually made up of five to nine wolves, but can be larger. The **dominant** members of the group are a partnered male and female. They **mate** only with each other in what is called a pair bond that usually lasts for life. The female has one litter per year. Other members of the pack are usually their offspring. Most of the offspring will leave to form packs of their own when they reach adulthood.

CHIMPANZEE COMMUNITIES

Chimpanzees live in large groups called communities, which live in and defend a **territory.** Chimps form smaller loose groups within these communities. The whole community is organized into a **dominance hierarchy,** so larger males and older females usually dominate these groups. Dominant females support their daughters so that they often gain high status, too. Social **grooming**—as well as some fighting—strengthens the order. The community will also fight to defend its territory from other chimpanzees.

CHANGING GROUPS

Many animal groups regularly change their **social structures** to avoid inbreeding. Inbreeding is when closely related animals breed together, often producing offspring with disease or birth defects. In chimpanzees and some bird flocks, females leave their communities to join another when they reach adulthood. Wolves form new packs with unrelated partners. In large grazing herds, it is generally the males that move to other groups to avoid inbreeding.

A parental pair leads a wolf pack.

Keeping order

Parakeets are parrots that live in flocks based around mating pairs. The groups have a pecking order that is kept in place by one bird pushing another off its perch, for example. But these smart birds remember their place in the pecking order and choose their fights carefully. They usually only try to push around birds that are close to their level in the order.

Parakeet flocks work together to find food.

Orca Pods

Orcas, also called killer whales, are the largest members of the dolphin family. These meat-eating ocean **mammals** live in groups called pods and hunt in cooler ocean waters. Depending on where the pod lives, it may prey on fish, seals, or other whale **species.**

Orca pods range in size from two to dozens of animals. A pod usually is made up of a **matriarch** and other individuals directly related to her. Male offspring stay in the group for life. Daughters may form new groups to raise their young but stay in the same area as their birth pod. Because a female orca may live to be as old as 50, family bonds stretch for several generations. Pods mix with others to breed. Orcas do not usually fight with each other, whether they are from the same pod or different pods.

Members of an orca pod communicate with each other constantly using different clicks, whistles, and calls. Each pod has its own special calls, which have been described as **dialects.** The orcas' clicks are used for echolocation, which is finding objects in the water by the way the sound bounces off them. This is one way the orcas find their **prey.**

Orcas, like other dolphins, hunt **schooling** fish. They may stun the fish with their tails before eating them. For larger prey, such as whales or dolphins, a pod swims in a way to reduce **drag** (see page 10) to chase its prey until it is exhausted. If the prey is a mammal, the pod traps it beneath the water so that it drowns. If a pod finds seals on an ice floe, it charges the floe as a tight group. This creates a wave that washes the seals into the water—right to the waiting orcas.

Ways to hunt are passed down through a pod from generation to generation. Young orcas learn the ways to hunt by watching the pod catch prey and by practicing as they get older.

Some ORCAS ride waves up onto a beach to grab a seal before slipping back into the sea.

Temporary Gatherings

Animal gatherings are often temporary. Animals that live by themselves or in smaller groups may come together in larger groups to **mate** or migrate. Sometimes it may simply be for added security and warmth while sleeping.

COMMUNAL ROOSTING

While many birds **forage** for food alone during the day, they often settle down together to sleep in **roosts.** They share body warmth and protect one another. These are the reasons why large groups of starlings and red-winged blackbirds, for example, often form at dusk. Roosts vary in size, with larger groups forming in the winter. A winter roost of red-winged blackbirds can be made up of several million individuals. Other **species** mix in with them. The birds split up in the morning, traveling distances of up to 50 miles (80 kilometers) as they feed, before gathering again in the evening.

INSECT ROOSTS

Some **insects,** especially butterflies, are known to form night roosts for safety. The red postman butterfly, which is found in cooler forest areas from the southwestern U.S. state of Texas down to South America, comes together in groups of about 10 on dry stems above the ground. **Zoologists** studying butterfly roosts found that birds were much more likely to prey on lone butterflies at night, rather than on those in roosts.

Chalkhill blue butterflies roost together for protection.

Red-winged blackbirds roosting together.

Daytime roosts

Bats mostly move about at night. They often form large **colonies** in caves, which they leave at dusk to start feeding. In some caves, the day **roosts** of the Brazilian free-tailed bat can contain more than a million individuals. A mother bat leaves its single offspring behind in a cave, but amazingly finds it again when it comes back.

Brazilian free-tailed bats roost during the day in dark, dry places, such as caves.

MIGRATION

Some animals form groups to make their seasonal migrations, often traveling huge distances to warmer or cooler climates. Animals migrate to make sure they have a constant food supply and favorable conditions for raising their young.

GATHERING BIRDS

Small birds called barn swallows migrate in flocks in the late summer from North America, where they breed (make more animals like themselves). They head south for the winter, sometimes traveling as far as the South American country of Argentina. The birds cover as much as 200 miles (320 kilometers) a day before stopping to **roost** for the night. No one knows for sure how the birds find their way, but scientists think that older birds guide younger ones in the flock. The journey is difficult: many birds die of starvation and exhaustion along the way.

OTHER MIGRATIONS

Birds are not the only type of animal to migrate in groups. Fish, such as sardines and herrings, **school** in huge numbers to warmer waters during some parts of the year in search of food (see page 39). Monarch butterflies form groups to migrate south in the winter. This journey spans many generations: along the way, millions of butterflies hatch, **reproduce,** and die. In winter, humpback whales swim south together, following the coasts, to warmer breeding grounds to raise their young. Many grazing animals have seasonal migrations. Wildebeests, zebras, and Thomson's gazelles travel across the African **savanna,** following seasonal rains in search of better grass to eat.

Caribou herds

Caribou migrate farther than any other land **mammal.** Some herds cover as much as 3,000 miles (4,800 kilometers) to reach their summer feeding grounds in the Arctic. Once among the lush summer grass, the herd size can swell to tens of thousands.

Caribou have the longest migration of any land mammal.

Millions of monarch butterflies migrate up to 2,970 miles (4,750 kilometers) each year.

MATING SEASON

Most animals make more animals like themselves through sexual **reproduction.** This means their offspring are formed from the **egg** of a female and the **sperm** of male. Animals have different ways of finding **mates** to reproduce, one of which is to come together in large groups. This often happens at a particular time of year, referred to as the mating season.

During the mating season, male bullfrogs gather at night by lakes and ponds. Each frog marks out a **territory** inside of these gatherings, calling out to warn other males off and to attract females. The female chooses a mate, laying her eggs in the water of his territory, which he then **fertilizes.** Males may call for over a month, adjusting their calls in relation to other males around them. They may mate with several females.

Atlantic salmon are fish that hatch in rivers but swim out to the ocean when they are two or three years old. They grow quickly at sea. After a year or two, they return to their home river to reproduce. The journey back upstream is hard. Many salmon die of exhaustion or are eaten by **predators** along the way. Survivors gather in pools to find a mate. The female digs a nest in the river bottom and lays her eggs in it, which the male then fertilizes. They may create several nests. Most of the adults then die, exhausted by the reproduction process. A few individuals manage to return to the sea.

Starting a swarm

Insects called desert locusts come in two forms: solitary and swarming locusts. When solitary locusts mate, the female tries to lay her eggs close to those of others. When the eggs hatch, the locusts spread out if food is plentiful. But if food is short, a chemical in the locusts' bodies triggers a change that makes the insects stay together. They become swarming locusts, actively looking for other locusts and searching for food. They breed again and can form huge groups, sometimes of over a billion individuals. These **swarms** can destroy crops.

Desert locusts are a type of grasshopper. An especially large swarm of locusts is called a plague.

BREEDING COLONIES

Birds often come together in groups to find a **mate.** Male and female members of some **species** then stay together as pairs, forming **colonies** of nests where they raise their chicks together. Land birds, such as swallows, form breeding colonies. This behavior is very common in seabirds, including penguins and gulls. Birds usually return to the same nesting place each year. Other animals, such as seals, also form breeding colonies.

Flightless penguins spend much of their time swimming in the oceans of the Southern Hemisphere. They come onto land to mate and raise their young, forming huge nesting colonies. King penguins form colonies of tens of thousands of pairs. Unusually, they build no nests. Instead, parents hold the single **egg** on their feet. First, the male holds the egg, then the female, while the other returns to the sea to feed. This shared parenting continues once the chick is hatched. When it is old enough, parents leave their chick with others in the colony and both go to find food.

COLONY ADVANTAGES

As in other large groups, nesting colonies give some protection from **predators** (see page 6). If a member of the colony senses a threat, it will tell the other members through its actions or calls. Birds will act together to drive away predators. For example, birds yellow-rumped caciques (kuh SEEKS) of Peru attack predators from the air as a group. Chicks have a greater chance of survival in a colony partly because they all hatch at once. Predators have so much food available at one time that they can only eat a small fraction of the chicks—most of them survive.

King penguins form large breeding colonies on Antarctic islands.

Invasive predators

Many seabird colonies are found on far-away islands, meaning that they have few predators. But such colonies can quickly be destroyed by **invasive species.** Rats have made it to many islands from ships and boats. Rats eat both eggs and chicks, and their numbers can grow quickly since there is so much food on breeding colony islands. The parent birds do not know how to keep the rats away. On the Abrolhos Islands, off the coast of the South American country of Brazil, the red-billed tropicbirds are in danger of **extinction** because of invasive rats.

The black rat, introduced in the 1800's to the U.S. island state of Hawaii, in the Pacific Ocean, preys on the chicks and eggs of native forest birds.

Raising Young

There are many advantages to raising young when living as part of a group. Along with many nesting birds, some animal groups build shelters.

BEAVER LODGES

Beavers live by water in small family groups called **colonies.** A colony is usually made up of about eight beavers: an adult pair (who **mate** for life) and their young of different ages—much smaller than the colonies of birds and **insects.** A new beaver couple builds a lodge of sticks, grass, and moss—stuck together with mud—just above the waterline to make a warm, dry place to raise their young. They sometimes build a dam around the lodge to protect it from fast-flowing water. Once a family is started, the whole colony works to keep up the lodge and dam.

BURROW NETWORKS

Prairie dogs are one of several kinds of small **mammals** that create networks of burrows, often called warrens. Family groups dig out these networks together, close to others, and spend a lot of time keeping them up. Most burrows have at least two openings surrounded by mounds of soil. The mounds protect burrows from flooding, improve airflow, and give prairie dogs raised perches to watch for **predators.** Young pups play outside the burrow, but quickly retreat to its safety if they hear an alarm call.

Caterpillar nest

Most moths lay their **eggs** in batches on plants so that when their caterpillars hatch they can eat the plants as food. Some moth caterpillars, such as the small ermine or small eggar moths, spin webs around the plants they hatch on. The webs protect these **larvae** from predators, such as birds, while they feed. If these webs are close together, they create silky curtains over the bushes.

Some moth caterpillars create protective webs around themselves.

Beaver colonies work together to build a lodge and dam.

Sociable Weavers

Weavers are birds famous for the complex hanging nests they build. Of the weaver **species,** perhaps the most amazing nest builder is the sociable weaver of South Africa. These birds build the biggest nests in the world, using sticks and grass. The roof alone can measure 25 feet (7.6 meters) long and 15 feet (4.6 meters) wide. Below it hang chambers (rooms), each of which is home to a breeding pair. As many as 100 individual nests can be found under one roof.

Some nests have been in use for over 100 years. A lot of birds will have lived there in that time. A breeding pair may raise as many as four families a year. This high **reproduction** rate is made possible by the warm, steady climate of their **habitat,** which enables it to have a good supply of food. Many chicks are victims of **predators,** such as snakes, but those that survive may live as long as ten years. Birds do not start families of their own until they are two or three years old. Until then, they stay in the nests, helping raise other chicks. For example, they keep the chambers lined with soft grass.

The nests are generally built and kept up by the males of the **colony.** They start with the roof, building it from larger sticks, then weave the linked chambers below from softer grass. Tunnels

SOCIABLE WEAVER
nests can weigh as much
as 2,000 pounds
(450 kilograms).

lead into the center of the nest from the outside. The birds protect these tunnels from predators by weaving spiky straws around them. Birds make the nest bigger over time and spend a lot of time keeping it in order. The group effort creates a safe, comfortable home for the birds to raise their young over many generations.

SHARED PARENTING

Among animals that live in groups, mothers (and sometimes fathers) usually care for their own young. But sometimes others in the group share in caring and protecting the young animals. Elephant herds work together to raise and protect their young. Female elephants will look after the newborn calves of the group, even if they are not their own offspring. For young elephants that are not old enough to **reproduce,** this "babysitting" gives them valuable practice at being a mother. When the herd senses danger, all members work to protect the calves by forming a ring around them. Musk oxen (see page 15) also work together in this way to defend the group's young.

PACK SUPPORT

Sometimes, group members help care for young by giving them food. In wolf packs, the **dominant** female (see page 18) gives birth to as many as 11 pups at once in the spring. At first, she cares for them on her own in the den she has dug, feeding them on her milk. But when the pups are about three weeks old, they can eat meat, so the rest of the pack helps feed them. First, pack members **regurgitate** meat they have already eaten for the pups. As the pups grow older, they are brought fresh meat. By winter, the young wolves begin hunting with the pack, playing small parts at first as they improve their skills.

NURSERY POOLS

Galápagos sea lions gather on the beaches of the Galápagos Islands to **mate.** A **harem** of about 30 females is protected by a single male. He keeps other males and possible **predators** away while the females give birth. Mothers leave their pups in shallow pools while the mothers return to the sea to find food. Other females take turns watching over the pups in this nursery.

Helper birds

The green wood hoopoe (HOO poo) is a common bird of **sub-Saharan Africa.** The birds live in groups where only one pair breeds. The father and the other "helper" birds bring the mother food, such as **insects,** which she then feeds to the chicks.

Green wood hoopoes raise their chicks with the support of helper birds.

A female Galápagos sea lion with her pup.

LEARNING FROM THE GROUP

Some animals survive on their own from the moment they are born. Most animals raised in groups receive care from parents or their group until they can be on their own. Some of the skills they need for survival may be innate (they are born with them), but others will be learned from the group.

HUNTING AND FORAGING

Wolves teach their young to hunt, as do orca pods (see page 20). Elephant **matriarchs** pass on their knowledge of where to find food to their calves. Chimpanzees are one of the few animals that use tools to find food— for example, some use a stick to pull **insects** from holes. Others use stones to crack open nuts. Young chimpanzees learn how to use these tools from their community, passing the skill from one generation to the next. The fact that different communities use tools in different ways shows that these activities are learned.

GROUP COMMUNICATION

Just as humans learn **language** from their parents, many animals learn to communicate from their group. Elephants signal to each other with their trunk and ears, using learned gestures, some special to their herd. Orca pods have their own **dialects,** as do chimpanzee communities. In some kinds of flocking birds, such as starlings and crows, each group has its own special songs and calls. These shared dialects help individuals identify other members of their group and keep in contact. They strengthen the bonds of the group.

Chimpanzees in a community learn to use different tools. Here, a female chimp and her young are using sticks to catch termites.

Animal cultures

Culture is the shared knowledge and behavior of a group that develops over many generations. We usually associate it with human groups. Many **zoologists** feel that some animal groups have their own cultures, because they have special, learned behaviors that are passed on from one generation to the next.

The learned behavior of an elephant herd is sometimes called its culture.

Downsides to Group Living

Although there are many good things about living in groups, there are downsides as well. Disease, competition for food and **mates,** and more attention from **predators** all reduce the benefit of living in a group.

ATTRACTING PREDATORS

While living in a group may help its members be more wary of predators, group living may also attract more predators. The grasslands of the African **savanna** are known not only for their huge herds of plant-eating animals, from zebras to wildebeests, but also the many animals that prey on them, such as cheetahs, hyenas, and lions. There are so many predators here because of the huge herds of potential **prey.**

FOOD SHORTAGES

Group living can sometimes help its members get food more easily, but it also creates more direct competition for it. Such competition becomes a problem when food is in short supply, due to droughts or poor weather or, in ocean **habitats,** water current changes. **Dominant** individuals may take their share first, leaving little or nothing for the other members of the group. The grasslands of Africa are often affected by drought. During these periods, many grazing animals, such as antelope, die. There is not enough water or plant life to keep up the herd's huge numbers. Also, herds of wild animals often have to compete with **livestock** herds for food resources.

Feeding frenzy

Some fish travel through the ocean in huge **schools,** often when they migrate (see page 24). From May to July, hundreds of millions of sardines swim up through the ocean waters along the east coast of Africa. This mass movement attracts many predators: dolphins, gannets, albatross, seals, whales, and sharks. The dolphins attack first, cutting off a group of fish. The group forms into a ball shape, which the dolphins force towards the surface. Then, other predators from the air as well as the water attack the ball.

Schooling sardines swim away from an attacking shark.

A spotted hyena stalks a herd of grazing wildebeest, picking out its prey.

COMPETITION FOR MATES

Some **social structures** may make it difficult for individual animals—usually males—to find a **mate.** When animals gather together to breed, males may fight with each other, sometimes injuring or killing one another. A **dominant** male may mate with all the females in the area and drive the other males away. Some males may come up with other ways to mate. They may **mimic** females to trick dominant males into allowing them to get close to real females. Other males may be much smaller and faster than dominant males so they can sneak by to mate with a female. At the **species** level, this competition is healthy. Some of the weaker males will be kept from mating, allowing the strongest—and sometimes, the sneakiest— males to **reproduce.**

DISEASES AND PARASITES

Diseases and **parasites,** too, can spread quickly around an animal group. Most need a single type of animal as a **host,** so a herd or pack offers far more chances to spread than what would be possible in lone individuals. Most of these diseases and parasites are not enough to kill an otherwise healthy animal, but they may weaken it, making it more likely to fall prey to **predators** or even bad weather. In the spring of 2015, over 200,000 saiga (*SY guh)* antelope died suddenly on the steppe grassland of the west-central Asian country of Kazakhstan—88 percent of the country's saiga population. The animals were killed by a blood infection. The infection is not usually so deadly, but the antelope were more easily affected by it because of unseasonably cold and windy weather. Female saiga give birth in the spring. The traumatic birthing process made females even more likely to get sick. Many mothers and their newborn calves died.

Parasite control

Animals in groups pass a lot of parasites between them. Lice hide in their fur and worms live in their guts. In some groups, such as communities of monkeys, animals **groom** each other's fur, picking out the parasites. This activity not only helps the group keep clean, but it also helps build social bonds.

Some macaque monkeys groom each other.

The saiga antelope, pictured here at a watering hole on the Russian steppe, is now critically endangered.

Insect Colonies

Eusocial insects form large, highly organized groups called **colonies.** In ants, wasps, and bees, a single female, called a queen, founds the colony. She starts building a nest, in which she lays her **eggs.** She will continue to lay eggs for the rest of her life. The first **larvae** to hatch from these eggs grow to become the female workers. They will never breed, but they make the nest bigger and find food for the queen, new larvae, and adult males. They also protect the colony. The males have one job: to **fertilize** the eggs of the queen.

BUILDING A COLONY

For most eusocial insects, the nest is the center of colony life. Ants may tunnel in the ground or build mounds with plant debris. Honey bees create a hive based around a honeycomb. Eusocial wasps make a nest from chewed wood. Wasps build a new nest each year, but honey bee hives and ant nests usually last much longer. As a queen bee gets older, worker bees will begin to raise new queens to replace her. They feed a few larvae a special diet, which causes them to grow into new queens. Ants, on the other hand, do not raise a replacement queen, so the colony dies when she dies. For both ants and bees, new queens leave the colony if it gets overcrowded. The queens leave the nest with the males in a **swarm** to **mate.** Each queen then starts a new colony.

Worker honey bees
keep up the hive.

A eusocial mammal

Very few **species** of **mammals** are eusocial. One of these is the naked mole-rat of eastern Africa. A single, breeding female leads the underground colony. The other females and most of the males do not breed. Only one or two males mate with the queen. The rest of the colony helps raise the young, and repair and protect their burrows.

Hairless naked mole-rats spend their entire life underground.

Male and new queen ants have wings so they can swarm.

The Termite Mound

There are many **species** of termite: some live in wood, some in soil. A few of the species in Africa and Australia that live in soil create gigantic nests, home to over a million **insects.** As part of these nests, they build huge towers of earth that can reach heights of over 20 feet (6 meters).

A termite **colony** is different from the colonies of other **eusocial** insects. At a termite colony's heart is a breeding pair—a king and queen. In larger colonies, there may be more than one pair. These breeding pairs produce workers and soldiers that can be male or female, but will never breed themselves. The small workers are the builders, caregivers, and **foragers.** The larger soldiers protect the nest from such **predators** as ants. Finally, a large colony has **reproductive** termites. Unlike the workers and soldiers, they have wings and will **swarm** short distances from the mound. They shed their wings, **mate,** and become the kings and queens of new colonies.

The workers build a mound with mud, which dries hard in the sun. Its surface has tiny holes that allows air and moisture to circulate in the chambers and passages inside the mound. These chambers and passages stretch several feet (over a meter) underground. In one chamber, the queen lays some 36,000 **eggs** per day. Cleaned and fed by tiny worker termites, the queen is the size of a human finger. The workers take the eggs to hatch in nearby nursery chambers.

A TERMITE mound in Kakadu National Park, Australia.

Some mound-building termites of Africa and Asia also grow **fungus** gardens. The workers place chewed-up grass and wood in garden chambers. The fungus converts the chewed-up material into sugars and other substances, which the termites eat for energy.

Glossary

camouflage the natural coloring or form of an animal that enables it to blend into its surroundings, making it difficult to see.

colony a group of living things of one species that live together or grow in the same place.

dialect a particular form of a communication method found in one specific region.

dominance hierarchy the structure found in some animal groups where one animal is dominant and others are submissive.

dominant having power or influence over another.

drag the force that pushes against an object when it moves through air or water, slowing it down.

egg a female sex cell, or the structure in which the embryo develops, usually outside the mother's body.

eusocial describes an animal that lives in a large, highly organized colony where only certain members reproduce and others animals cooperate to raise young and maintain the colony.

extinction when every member of a species (kind) of living thing has died.

fertilize to join sperm from a male with egg from a female so that a young animal develops.

foraging searching for food.

fungus (plural fungi) a living thing that usually grows on plants or on decaying matter. Yeast and mushrooms are fungi.

grooming when an animal cleans its own or another's feathers, fur, or skin.

habitat the place where a living thing usually makes its home.

harem in animals, a group of females controlled by a dominant male.

host a living thing that is either harmed or not affected in a symbiotic relationship. A symbiotic relationship is a relationship between two species from which at least one benefits.

insect one of the major invertebrate groups. Invertebrate animals do not have a backbone. Insects have six legs and a three-part body.

invasive species a type of living thing that spreads rapidly in a new environment where there are few or no natural controls on its growth.

language a system of communication where signs or signals (such as sounds) are connected together to create a specific meaning.

larva (plural larvae) the active, immature stage of some animals, such as many insects, that is different from its adult form.

livestock the animals farmers keep for their meat, milk, hides, or wool, such as sheep and goats.

mammal one of the major vertebrate animal groups. Vertebrate animals have a backbone. Mammals feed their offspring on milk produced by the mother, and most have hair or fur.

mate the animal with which another animal partners to reproduce; the act of mating, when two animals come together to reproduce.

matriarch a dominant mother that heads up an animal group.

mimic to copy something, or the close external resemblance of an animal to something else; an animal that does this.

mollusk a group of invertebrates that includes slugs, snails, mussels, and octopuses. Invertebrate animals do not have a backbone.

parasite a living thing that lives on or inside another living thing, such as an animal or plant, and gets its food from it.

predator an animal that hunts, kills, and eats other animals.

prey an animal that is hunted, killed, and eaten by

Find Out More

another.

regurgitate to bring food that has been swallowed back up into the mouth again.

reproduction the process by which living things produce their young, creating the next generation of their species, and passing on their genes.

reptile one of the major vertebrate animal groups. Vertebrate animals have a backbone. A reptile has dry, scaly skin and breathes air. Snakes, crocodiles, and lizards are all reptiles.

roost a place where a group of animals, particularly birds, regularly sleeps; the act of roosting.

savanna grasslands with widely scattered bushes and trees.

school in fish, to move together in a large group through the water; a group of fish moving together through the water.

shoal a group of fish.

social structure a network of relationships among individual animals and groups of animals.

species a group of living things that have certain permanent traits in common and are able to reproduce with each other.

sperm a male sex cell.

sub-Saharan Africa the part of Africa south of the Sahara Desert.

submissive yielding to the power, control, or authority of another individual.

swarm a large group of arthropods moving together either in search of food or a new home. An arthropod is an animal with jointed legs and no backbone.

territory an area of land or water controlled by an animal or group of animals, which they defend from other animals.

zoologist a scientist who studies animals.

BOOKS

Animal Armies (series title) by Richard and Louise Spilsbury (PowerKids, 2013)

Behavior in Living Things (The Web of Life) by Michael Bright (Raintree, 2012)

Family Groups (Animal Adaptations) by Simon Rose (Weigl Publishing, 2015)

WEBSITES

All About Lions
cbs.umn.edu/research/labs/lionresearch/all-about-lions
A website related to the long-term research of zoologists from the University of Minnesota into lions and their prides.

BBC Earth
bbc.com/earth/story/20161206-the-sad-fate-of-the-saiga-antelope-from-planet-earth-ii
BBC Earth explores the 2016 mass death of the saiga, which happened to take place when a BBC natural history program was being filmed there.

ElephantVoices
www.elephantvoices.org
The website of an organization built around long-term research into how elephant herds operate.

Jane Goodall Institute
www.janegoodall.org
Describes the work and research by Dr. Jane Goodall into chimpanzee communities, with information on the organization she founded to conserve them.

Orca Lab
orcalab.org/orcas/
The website of a Canadian research project into marine life, particularly orcas, off the Pacific coast of North America.

Index